SYDNEY 2000

THE OLYMPIC CITY

PROUDLY MADE IN AUSTRALIA

KEN DUNCAN
PANOGRAPHS®

The Sydney 2000 Olympic Games will be characterised by the vibrant qualities of Australia itself and the visionary hope felt at the turn of a new millennium. They will reflect the vitality, spontaneity, good humour and good nature of Australia.

The Mark of the Sydney 2000 Olympic Games echoes the sails of the Sydney Opera House, and the inspirational qualities of the Olympic torch. At the centre stands the athlete—the hero of the Games. The boomerang flies toward 2000 as a symbol of the Olympic athlete's skill.

The colours of the Sydney 2000 logo represent the elements—water (blue), earth (yellow) and air (red), which are also the colours of the Australian landscape.

The Olympic symbol consists of the five Olympic rings and represents the union of the five continents and the meeting of athletes from throughout the world at the Olympic Games.

TITLE PAGE
New Year's Eve fireworks, Sydney Harbour

LEFT
Sydney Harbour Bridge and Opera House at twilight

Dominated by its famous Harbour Bridge and Opera House, Sydney is without doubt one of the world's most beautiful cities. Its spectacular Harbour, golden beaches and temperate climate combine to make it a jewel in Australia's crown.

Harbour waters glistening in the sunlight like a million diamonds capture the city's essence of sparkling life.

Brisk and dynamic, Sydney is rich in history and brimming with a vibrant cosmopolitan culture. The great expanses of water that surround and run through the city create a wonderful sense of freedom in the middle of its busy life.

As the major gateway to Australia, Sydney welcomes innumerable travellers to one of the world's oldest and most mysterious continents.

DEDICATION
This book is dedicated to the most special person in my life, my wife Pamela.

PREVIOUS PAGE
Aerial view from Manly to the city

LEFT
Palm Beach and Barrenjoey Lighthouse, sunset

PREVIOUS PAGE
Beach life, Bondi

LEFT
Glebe Island Bridge, sunset

NEXT PAGE
*Australia Day celebrations,
Sydney Harbour*

PREVIOUS PAGE
Mahon Pool, Maroubra

RIGHT
Bondi Awakening

NEXT PAGE
Campbells Cove

PREVIOUS PAGE
Camp Cove and Watsons Bay

ABOVE AND RIGHT
Monorail, Darling Harbour

NEXT PAGE
Golden sands, Narrabeen Beach

Like a great boat under full sail, the Sydney Opera House rises majestically over the waters of Sydney Harbour. One of the city's best-known icons, this landmark is testimony to the beauty that can be created when architecture and environment unite as one.

The Harbour is like a highway tying this vast city together. Every morning, as traffic flows across the Bridge, water ferries arrive to disgorge thousands of commuters. Not far away, small inner harbour beaches nestle like precious havens. Historical buildings and parklands crowd its shores, and flotillas of yachts dot its blue waters. During community celebrations it explodes with colour, light and sound. The Harbour is truly the heart of Sydney.

RIGHT
Sydney Opera House at daybreak

NEXT PAGE
Parramatta River, Hunters Hill

Sydney abounds in glorious beaches. Stretching north and south of the city, these playgrounds by the sea are literally at people's front doors. Thousands enjoy an outdoor life of sand and sea.

In summer the beach is a riot of colour, surf, games, laughter, noise. Even in winter, there's nothing better than to start a day on the beach watching a glowing sunrise, or to end it watching a fiery sunset.

Living near water can give great clarity to our lives as nothing clutters the horizon. There's a permanence and purity to the ocean that balances and cleanses the city's soul. Like a wave catching a child's sandcastle, it catches us with its untamed loveliness.

RIGHT
Avalon Beach

NEXT PAGE
The Spit Bridge, Middle Harbour

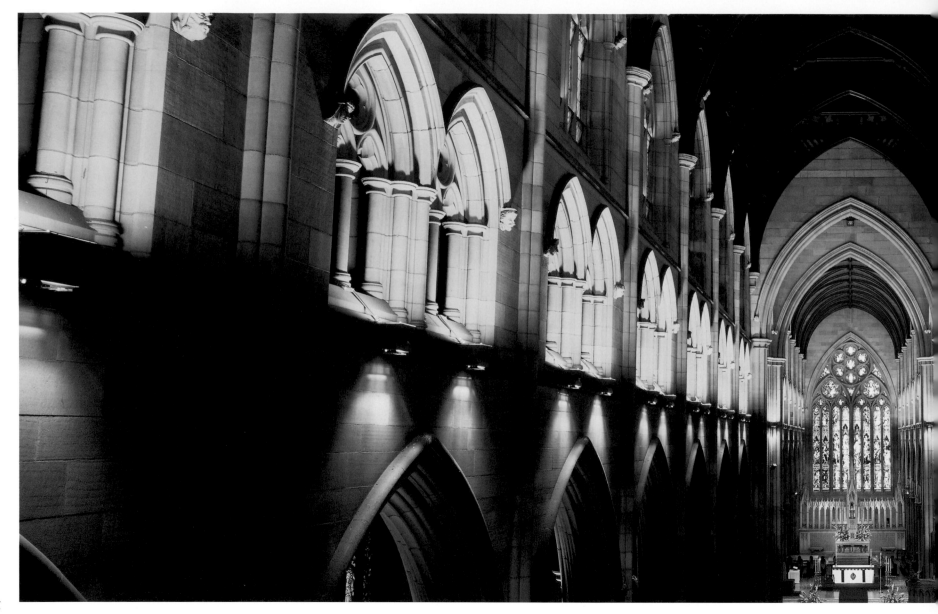

ABOVE
Time to reflect, Manly Cove

NEXT PAGE
A new day, Sydney Cove

SURFCRAFT PROHIBITED

LEFT
Sun seekers, Bronte Beach

NEXT PAGE
George Street, The Rocks

Shopping is one of the many great experiences to be enjoyed in Sydney. Out of the city's great multicultural mix, a vast array of shops offers anything one could ask for.

Many of these businesses are located in the striking nineteenth century sandstone buildings that pepper Sydney's streets. These buildings are not just architectural classics; they are part of the city's unique identity. Made from locally quarried rock, many have now been transformed by sensitive refurbishment and turned to modern uses—like the shopping mall in lovely old Queen Victoria Building.

In this way, the best achievements of the past are blended with the highest hopes for the future.

RIGHT
The Queen Victoria Building

PREVIOUS PAGE
Bondi from the air

ABOVE
Cityscape from Darling Harbour

SYDNEY 2000 - THE OLYMPIC CITY
First published in 1998
by Ken Duncan Panographs® Pty Limited
ACN 050 235 606
P.O. Box 3015, Wamberal NSW 2260,
Australia. Telephone: (02) 4367 6777.
www.kenduncan.com

Copyright photography and text:
© Ken Duncan 1998
Designed by Good Catch Design.
Edited by Owen Salter.
Colour separations by Purescript.
Printed by The Pot Still Press.
Bound by Podlich Enterprises.
Distributed by Gary Allen Pty Limited

The National Library of Australia
Cataloguing-in-Publication entry:
Duncan, Ken
Sydney 2000: the Olympic city.
ISBN 0 9586681 8 3.
1. Sydney (NSW) - Pictorial works. I. Title.
994.40222

TM©SOCOG 1996
http://socog.olympic.com.au